A Note to Parents and Teachers

DK READERS is a compelling reading programme for children, designed in conjunction with leading literacy experts, including Cliff Moon M.Ed., Honorary Fellow of the University of Reading. Cliff Moon has spent many years as a teacher and teacher educator specializing in reading and has written more than 160 books for children and teachers. He is series editor to Collins Big Cat.

Beautiful illustrations and superb full-colour photographs combine with engaging, easy-to-read stories to offer a fresh approach to each subject in the series. Each DK READER is guaranteed to capture a child's interest while developing his or her reading skills, general knowledge, and love of reading.

The five levels of DK READERS are aimed at different reading abilities, enabling you to choose the books that are exactly right for your child:

Pre-level 1: Learning to read
Level 1: Beginning to read
Level 2: Beginning to read alone
Level 3: Reading alone
Level 4: Proficient readers

The "normal" age at which a child begins to read can be anywhere from three to eight years old, so these levels are only a general guideline.

No matter which level you select, you can be sure that you are helping your child learn to read, then read to

LONDON, NEW YORK, MUNICH,
MELBOURNE, AND DELHI

Series Editor Deborah Lock
Art Editor Clare Shedden
Picture Researcher Liz Moore
Jacket Designer Emy Manby
Production Angela Graef
DTP Designer Almudena Díaz
Illustrator Peter Dennis
Subject Consultant Peter Bond

Reading Consultant
Cliff Moon, M.Ed.

Published in Great Britain by
Dorling Kindersley Limited
80 Strand, London WC2R 0RL

6 8 10 9 7

014-DD348-Aug/2006

A Penguin Company

A CIP record for this book is available
from the British Library
ISBN-13: 978-1-4053-1500-5

Colour reproduction by Colourscan, Singapore
Printed and bound in China by L. Rex Printing Co., Ltd.

The publisher would like to thank the following for their kind
permission to reproduce their photographs:
Position key: a-above; b-below/bottom; c-centre; l-left; r-right; t-top
Alamy Images: Mary Evans Picture Library 24tl, 25tr; Picture Contact
26b; Royal Geographical Society 7; **Norbert Aujoulat / Centre National
de la Recherche Scientifique / CNP-MCC**: 4; **www.bridgeman.co.uk**:
27t; British Library 17t; **Corbis**: Claudius / Zefa 11b; Stapleton Collection
9; **DK Images**: Anglo Australian Observatory 20; British Museum, London
17b; NASA 1, 30b, 30-31b; NASA / Hubble Heritage Team 21cl; **NASA**:
CXC/SAO 31t; ESA and The Hubble Heritage Team (STScI / AURA)
21cr, 21bl; H. Ford (JHU), G. Ilingworth (UCSC / LO), M. Clampin
(STScI), G. Hartig (STScI), the ACS Science Team, and ESA 21br;
Robert Williams and the Hubble Deep Field Team (STScI) 21t; **Science
Photo Library**: J-C Cuillandre / Canada-France-Hawaii Telescope 3; Dr
Fred Espenak 19b; MPIA-HD, BIRKLE, SLAWIK 12t; NASA 18-19t;
David Nunuk 5b, 32cra; John Sanford 32t; John Sanford & David Parker
11t; Jerry Schad 22b, 24-25b; Dr. Jurgen Scriba 32clb; Eckhard Slawik 5t,
10b, 15, 16, 23, 27b, 29tl, 29tr; Frank Zullo 14br, 28t
All other images © Dorling Kindersley
For more information see: www.dkimages.com

Contents

DK READERS

BEGINNING TO READ ALONE

2

Starry Sky

Written by Kate Hayden

DK

A Dorling Kindersley Book

On a clear, dark night, the sky
sparkles with thousands of stars.
These giant balls of gas make
their own heat and light
just like our closest star, the Sun.

Long ago, when people lived
in caves, they noticed patterns
among the brightest stars.
They made them into pictures.
If you look up into the sky,
you can see star patterns, too.

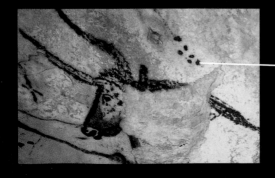

*Stars drawn
onto the wall
of a rock shelter
in France
16,500 years ago*

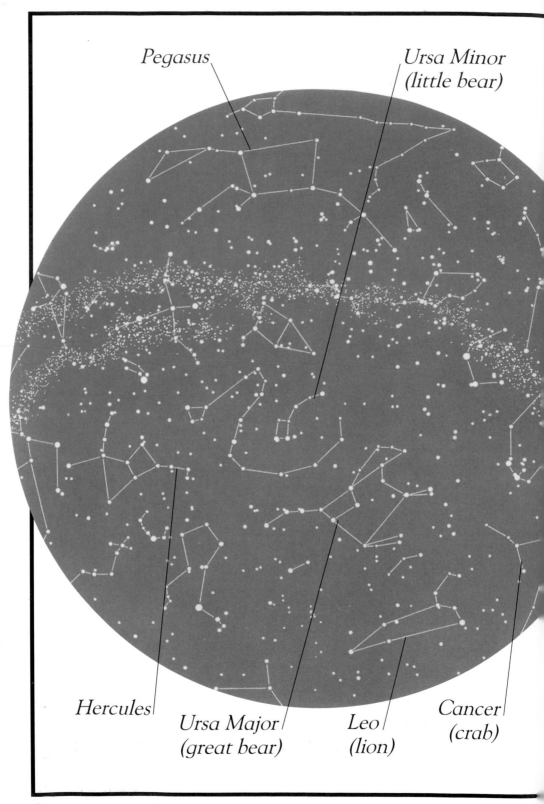

Pegasus

Ursa Minor
(little bear)

Hercules

Ursa Major
(great bear)

Leo
(lion)

Cancer
(crab)

Big star patterns are
called constellations
[KON-stuh-lay-shunz].
Star maps help you find
the constellations.

They tell you what star patterns
you can see at different times
of the year.

Star maps also show you
the different stars you can see
in different parts of the world.

The zodiac

The zodiac is a band of
12 constellations, such
as Leo and Cancer,
that the Sun appears to
pass through in a year.

Cancer the crab

There are 88 named constellations.
Some are named after animals, birds and fish.
Others have the names of people and creatures from legends.
There are some constellations named after objects, such as crowns and cups.
The names help people find stars in the night sky.

Corona
[kor-OH-nah]
the crown

Ursa Minor

Pegasus

Cancer

Leo

Ursa Major

Hercules

The Plough

The Ursa Major constellation

Many constellations have animal names, such as Ursa Major [ER-suh MAY-jer] the great bear, Leo the lion and Lupus the wolf. The constellation Taurus shows the front of a bull.

Bulls were important symbols for people in ancient times.

The Plough

A star pattern called the Plough, or the Big Dipper, links seven bright stars in Ursa Major.

The Taurus constellation

Apis, the Ancient Egyptian bull god

They made statues of them and worshipped them as gods.

*The Pleiades
star cluster on
the shoulder of
Taurus*

*The seven sisters
called the Pleiades*

Different cultures tell different
star stories.

In a Greek legend, the hunter
Orion chased seven sisters called
the Pleiades [PLEE-uh-deez].

The girls escaped from him
by turning into doves.
Finally, they became stars.

Navajo [NA-vuh-ho] Indians
call these seven stars
the Flint Boys.
Their sky god, Black God,
wore them on his ankle.
When he stamped
his foot, they bounced
onto his forehead
and stayed there.

The Flint Boys

*Navajo drawing
of Black God*

Orion [oh-RYE-un] the hunter is another well-known constellation. He carries a club, and a sword hangs from his belt.
Nearby is his hunting dog – the constellation Canis Major [KAH-niss MAY-jer] the great dog. The brightest star Sirius [SEER-ee-us], or the Dog Star, is found in this constellation.

Sirius

The Canis Major constellation

Orion the
hunter

Orion's belt

The Orion constellation

Cepheus
[SEE-fee-us]

Cassiopeia
[kass-ee-oh-PEE-uh]

Perseus
[PURR-see-us]

Andromeda
[an-DROH-me-duh]

The W-shaped constellation is
called Cassiopeia.

In a Greek story, she is the wife
of King Cepheus and they have
a daughter named Andromeda.

*Perseus killing
the sea monster Cetus*

Andromeda was chained to a rock, waiting to be eaten by the sea monster Cetus [SEE-tus]. The Greek hero Perseus flew down on the winged horse, Pegasus, and saved Andromeda.

Pegasus

The winged horse, Pegasus, appears in many Greek stories. He was shown on Ancient Greek coins, vases and other objects.

Earth is more than one million times smaller than the Sun.

Faraway stars look small and vary in brightness.

Close-up, they are enormous, fiery balls of gas.

The Sun is our nearest star.

Explosions in the Sun's scorching core make it shine.

Huge flares jumping into space from the Sun

Star colours
The hottest stars are blue and the coolest are red. In between are white, yellow and orange stars.

The sizzling surface simmers like milk bubbling in a saucepan. Heat and light escape into space from the surface.

A spiral galaxy

In our galaxy, the Sun is in one of the spiral arms.

Most stars belong to giant
star groups called galaxies.
The Sun is one of at least
100 billion stars in
the Milky Way galaxy.
This galaxy has a spiral shape.

There are many
other galaxies
in the universe.
Some are spiral
with a bar of stars across the middle.
Others are shaped like tadpoles,
rings or even Mexican hats!

Sombrero (Mexican hat) galaxy

Barred-spiral galaxy

Ring galaxy

Tadpole galaxy

A Chinese story
says that the star
Vega was
Chih Nu,
the gods' weaving girl, and the star
Altair was Niu Lang, a cowherd.
When Chih Nu married Niu Lang,
the angry gods separated them
with a river, the Milky Way.

The Milky Way
From Earth, our galaxy
is seen on its side.
The light from the
distant stars looks
like a river of milk.

Vega

The Milky Way
separates the
two stars.

Altair

On Chinese Valentine's Day,
the Milky Way appears dimmer.
On this one day, Chih Nu
and Niu Lang are not separated.

The eagle

Altair is found in the
constellation of Aquila
the eagle. In stories,
this bird belonged to
the Greek god Zeus.

Altair

Altair, Vega and a star called
Deneb form the Summer Triangle.
Deneb is 25 times larger and shines
60,000 times stronger than the Sun.

Deneb

The Cygnus constellation

Vega

Deneb means "tail" in Arabic.
This distant star can be seen
on the tail of the constellation
Cygnus [SIG-nus] the swan.

Stars have often helped people
in their daily lives.
In Egypt, people realised that
when the star Sirius rose before
the Sun in summer, the River Nile
would soon flood.
They needed the flood for growing
healthy crops in their fields.

A traveller finding his position from a star

In the past, sailors and other travellers used special tools to look at stars for checking their position and finding their way.

Starry signposts

Two stars in the Southern Cross point to the South Pole. The North Star is seen above the North Pole.

Sirius, the brightest star in the night sky

On a clear night we can see thousands of stars, and with special equipment we can see even more.

Sirius seen through binoculars

Sirius seen through a strong telescope

With binoculars, we can see
tens of thousands of stars.
With a small telescope,
we can see millions of stars.
Astronomers – people
who study the stars –
use powerful telescopes.

Powerful telescopes have been
put into space to discover
more about the universe.
The Hubble Space Telescope
orbits the Earth.
It provides very detailed images
of faraway galaxies.

*Hubble Space
Telescope*

*Chandra X-ray
Observatory*

The Chandra X-ray Observatory
picks up X-rays – light that is
invisible to us – from the stars.

In the future, who knows
what else we will discover in
the mysterious starry sky. . .

Starry facts

There are more stars in the universe than grains of sand on all of the beaches on Earth.

Astronomers measure how far away stars are in light-years. A light-year is the distance light can travel in a year – about 9 trillion km (5.88 trillion miles). The star Sirius is eight and a half light-years away.

A shooting star is not really a star. It is actually a meteor – a piece of comet dust falling from space.

An observatory is where astronomers observe the night sky. In the mountains of Chile, where the skies are very clear, four separate telescopes work together to get amazing images of the universe.

A planisphere is a star map that has a rotating window. The window is lined up with the date and time of night to show the stars that can be seen.